ABDU'L-BAHA IN LONDON

The City Temple: Introduction

ON September 10th, the first Sunday after Abdu'l-Baha's arrival in England, he spoke from the City Temple pulpit to the evening congregation at the special desire of the Pastor, the Reverend R. J. Campbell.

Though Abdu'l-Baha's coming had not been advertised the Church was filled to its utmost capacity. Few that were there will ever forget the sight of that venerable figure clad in his Eastern garb, ascending the pulpit stairs to address a public gathering for the first time in his life. That this should be at a Christian place of worship in the West has its own deep significance. Mr. Campbell introduced the visitor with a few simple words in the course of which he said: "We, as the followers of the Lord Jesus Christ, who is to us and will always be the Light of the World, view with sympathy and respect every movement of the Spirit of God in the experience of mankind, and therefore we give greeting to Abdu'l-Baha in the name of all who share the spirit of our Master, and are trying to live their lives in that Spirit. The Baha'i Movement is very closely akin to, I think I might say is identical with, the spiritual purpose of Christianity."

Before Abdu'l-Baha left the Church, he wrote in the old Bible used by generations of preachers, the following words in his own native Persian, the translation being added as follows:

Inscription in the Old Bible

Written by Abdu'l-Baha in Persian

THIS book is the Holy Book of God, of celestial Inspiration. It is the Bible of Salvation, the Noble Gospel. It is the mystery of the Kingdom and its light. It is the Divine Bounty, the sign of the guidance of God.

Address given by Abdu'l-Baha at the City Temple

Sunday, September 10th, 1911

O NOBLE friends; seekers after God! Praise be to God! Today the light of Truth is shining upon the world in its abundance; the breezes of the heavenly garden are blowing throughout all regions; the call of the Kingdom is heard in all lands, and the breath of the Holy Spirit is felt in all hearts that are faithful. The Spirit of God is giving eternal life. In this wonderful age the East is enlightened, the West is fragrant, and everywhere the soul inhales the holy perfume. The sea of the unity of mankind is lifting up its waves with joy, for there is real communication between the hearts and minds of men. The banner of the Holy Spirit is uplifted, and men see it, and are assured with the knowledge that this is a new day.

This is a new cycle of human power. All the horizons of the world are luminous, and the world will become indeed as a garden and a paradise. It is the hour of unity of the sons of men and of the drawing together of all races and all classes. You are loosed from ancient superstitions which have kept men ignorant, destroying the foundation of true humanity.

The gift of God to this enlightened age is the knowledge of the oneness of mankind and of the fundamental oneness of religion. War shall cease between nations, and by the will of God the Most Great Peace shall come; the world will be seen as a new world, and all men will live as brothers.

In the days of old an instinct for warfare was developed in the struggle with wild animals; this is no longer necessary; nay, rather, co-operation and mutual understanding are seen to produce the greatest welfare of mankind. Enmity is now the result of prejudice only.

In the Hidden Words Baha'u'llah says, "Justice is to be loved above all." Praise be to God, in this country the standard of justice has been raised; a great effort is being made to give all souls an equal and a true place. This is the desire of all noble natures; this is today the teaching for the East and for the West; therefore the East and the West will understand each other and reverence each other, and embrace like long-parted lovers who have found each other.

There is one God; mankind is one; the foundations of religion are one. Let us worship Him, and give praise for all His great Prophets and Messengers who have manifested His brightness and glory.

The blessing of the Eternal One be with you in all its richness, that each soul according to his measure may take freely of Him. Amen.

This Address is printed by kind permission, from The Christian Commonwealth of September 13th, 1911. Spoken by Abdu'l-Baha in Persian from the city Temple pulpit, the above translation was then read to the congregation by Mr. W. Tudor-Pole.

St. John's Westminster: Introduction

On September 17th, Abdu'l-Baha at the request of the venerable Archdeacon of Westminster addressed the congregation of Saint John the Divine after evening service. With a few warm words characteristic of his whole attitude Archdeacon Wilberforce introduced the revered Messenger from the East, who had crossed seas and countries on his Mission of Peace and Unity for which he had suffered forty years of captivity and persecution. The Archdeacon had the Bishop's chair placed for his Guest on the Chancel steps, and standing beside him read the translation of Abdu'l-Baha's address himself. The Congregation was profoundly moved, and following the Archdeacon's example knelt to receive the blessing of the Servant of God--who stood with extended arms--his wonderful voice rising and falling in the silence with the power of his invocation. As the Archdeacon said: "Truly the East and the West have met in this sacred place tonight." The hymn "O God our help in ages past" was sung by the entire assembly standing, as Abdu'l-Baha and the Archdeacon passed down the aisle to the vestry hand in hand.

Outside the Church, Salvationists were holding their meeting and Abdu'l-Baha was deeply impressed and touched at the sight of the men, women and children gathered together in the night, at the street corner, praying and singing.

Discourse of Abdu'l-Baha at St. John's,

Westminster.

September 17th, 1911.

O NOBLE Friends! O Seekers for the Kingdom of God! Man all over the world is seeking for God. All that exists is God; but the Reality of Divinity is holy above all understanding.

The pictures of Divinity that come to our mind are the product of our fancy; they exist in the realm of our imagination. They are not adequate to the Truth; truth in its essence cannot be put into words.

Divinity cannot by comprehended because it is comprehending.

Man, who has also a real existence, is comprehended by God; therefore, the Divinity which man can understand is partial; it is not complete. Divinity is actual Truth and real existence, and not any representation of it. Divinity itself contains All, and is not contained.

Although the mineral, vegetable, animal and man all have actual being, yet the mineral has no knowledge of the vegetable. It cannot apprehend it. It cannot imagine nor understand it.

It is the same with the vegetable. Any progress it may make, however highly it may become developed, it will never apprehend the animal, nor understand it. It is, so to speak, without news of it. It has no ears, no sight, no understanding.

It is the same with the animal. However much it may progress in its own kingdom, however refined its feelings may become, it will have no real notion of the world of man or of his special intellectual faculties.

The animal cannot understand the roundness of the earth, nor its motion in space, nor the central position of the sun, nor can it imagine such a thing as the all-pervading ether.

Although the mineral, vegetable, animal and man himself are actual beings, the difference between their kingdoms prevents members of the lower degree from comprehending the essence and nature of those of the superior degree. This being so, how can the temporal and phenomenal comprehend the Lord of Hosts?

It is clear that this is impossible!

But the Essence of Divinity, the Sun of Truth, shines forth upon all horizons and is spreading its rays upon all things. Each creature is the recipient of some portion of that power, and man, who contains the perfection of the mineral, the vegetable and animal, as well as his own distinctive qualities, has become the noblest of created beings. It stands written that he is made in the Image of God. Mysteries that were hidden he discovers; and secrets that were concealed he brings into the light. By Science and by Art he brings hidden powers into the region of the visible world. Man perceives the hidden law in created things and co-operates with it.

Lastly the perfect man, the Prophet, is one who is transfigured, one who has the purity and clearness of a perfect mirror--one who reflects the Sun of Truth. Of such a one--of such a Prophet and Messenger--we can say that the Light of Divinity with the heavenly Perfections dwells in him.

If we claim that the sun is seen in the mirror, we do not mean that the sun itself has descended from the holy heights of his heaven and entered into the mirror! This is impossible. The Divine Nature is seen in the Manifestations and its Light and Splendor are visible in extreme glory.

Therefore, men have always been taught and led by the Prophets of God. The Prophets of God are the Mediators of God. All the Prophets and Messengers have come from One Holy Spirit and bear the Message of God, fitted to the age in which they appear. The One Light is in them and they are One with each other. But the Eternal does not become phenomenal; neither can the phenomenal become Eternal.

Saint Paul, the great Apostle, said: "We all, with open face beholding as in a mirror the glory of God, are changed into the same image from glory to glory, as by the Spirit of the Lord."

O GOD the Forgiver! O Heavenly Educator! This assembly is adorned with the mention of thy holy Name. Thy children turn their face towards thy Kingdom, hearts are made happy and souls are comforted.

Merciful God! cause us to repent of our shortcomings! Accept us in thy heavenly Kingdom and give unto us an abode where there shall be no error. Give us peace; give us knowledge, and open unto us the gates of thy heaven.

Thou art the Giver of all! Thou art the Forgiver! Thou art the Merciful! Amen.

Theosophical Society: Introduction

ON September 30th, Abdu'l-Baha met the Theosophical society at their new Headquarters at the express request of their president Mrs. Annie Besant. After a general history of the movement and sympathetic words of welcome by Mr. A. P. Sinnett, Abdu'l-Baha rose and delivered to the crowded assembly an address upon the distinctive notes of the Baha'i teaching, warmly commending the eagerness of the Society in its search for Truth.

Discourse of Abdu'l-Baha given at the

Theosophical Head Quarters.

September 30th, 1911.

O RESPECTED Assembly! O friends of Truth! The inherent nature of fire is to burn, the inherent nature of electricity is to give light, the inherent nature of the sun is to shine, and the inherent nature of the organic earth is the power of growth.

There is no separation between a thing and its inherent qualities.

It is the inherent nature of things on this earth to change, thus we see around us the change of the seasons. Every spring is followed by a summer and every autumn brings a winter--every day a night and every evening a morning. There is a sequence in all things.

Thus when hatred and animosity, fighting, slaughtering, and great coldness of heart were governing this world, and darkness had overcome the nations, Baha'u'llah, like a bright star, rose from the horizon of Persia and shone with the great Light of Guidance, giving heavenly radiance and establishing the new Teaching.

He declared the most human virtues; He manifested the Spiritual powers, and put them into practice in the world around Him.

Firstly: He lays stress on the search for Truth. This is most important, because the people are too easily led by tradition. It is because of this that they are often antagonistic to each other, and dispute with one another.

But the manifesting of Truth discovers the darkness and becomes the cause of Oneness of faith and belief: because Truth cannot be two! That is not possible.

Secondly: Baha'u'llah taught the Oneness of humanity; that is to say, all the children of men are under the mercy of the Great God. They are the sons of one God; they are trained by God. He has placed the crown of humanity on the head of every one of the servants of God. Therefore all nations and peoples must consider themselves brethren. They are all descendants from Adam. They are the branches, leaves, flowers and fruits of One Tree. They are pearls from one shell. But the children of men are in need of education and civilization, and they require to be polished, till they become bright and shining.

Man and woman both should be educated equally and equally regarded.

It is racial, patriotic, religious and class prejudice, that has been the cause of the destruction of Humanity.

Thirdly: Baha'u'llah taught, that Religion is the chief foundation of Love and Unity and the cause of Oneness. If a religion become the cause of hatred and disharmony, it would be better that it should not exist. To be without such a religion is better than to be with it.

Fourthly: Religion and Science are inter-twined with each other and cannot be separated. These are the two wings with which humanity must fly. One wing is not enough. Every religion which does not concern itself with Science is mere tradition, and that is not the essential. Therefore science, education and civilization are most important necessities for the full religious life.

Fifthly: The Reality of the divine Religions is one, because the Reality is one and cannot be two. All the prophets are united in their message, and unshaken. They are like the sun; in different seasons they ascend from different rising points on the horizon. Therefore every ancient prophet gave the glad tidings of the future, and every future has accepted the past.

Sixthly: Equality and Brotherhood must be established among all members of mankind. This is according to Justice. The general rights of mankind must be guarded and preserved.

All men must be treated equally. This is inherent in the very nature of humanity.

Seventhly: The arrangements of the circumstances of the people must be such that poverty shall disappear, and that every one as far as possible, according to his position and rank, shall be comfortable. Whilst the nobles and others in high rank are in easy circumstances, the poor also should be able to get their daily food and not be brought to the extremities of hunger.

Eighthly: Baha'u'llah declared the coming of the Most Great Peace. All the nations and peoples will come under the shadow of the Tent of the Great Peace and Harmony--that is to say, by general election a Great Board of Arbitration shall be established, to settle all differences and quarrels between the Powers; so that disputes shall not end in war.

Ninthly: Baha'u'llah taught that hearts must receive the Bounty of the Holy Spirit, so that Spiritual civilization may be established. For material civilization is not adequate for the needs of mankind and cannot be the cause of its happiness. Material civilization is like the body and spiritual civilization is like the soul. Body without soul cannot live.

This is a short summary of the Teachings of Baha'u'llah. To establish this Baha'u'llah underwent great difficulties and hardships. He was in constant confinement and He suffered great persecution. But in the fortress (Akka) He reared a spiritual palace and from the darkness of His prison He sent out a great light to the world.

It is the ardent desire of the Baha'is to put these teachings into common practice: and they will strive with soul and heart to give up their lives for this purpose, until the heavenly light brightens the whole world of humanity.

I am very happy that I have been able to talk with you in this gathering: and hope that this deep consciousness of mine is acceptable to you.

I pray for you, that you may succeed in your aspirations and that the bounties of the Kingdom may be yours.

Farewell Reception: Introduction

On the evening of St. Michael's day, a large farewell reception was given to Abdu'l-Baha in the hall of the Passmore Edwards' Settlement, which was filled to its utmost capacity with representative people of every profession, some coming from great distances.

On the platform surrounding Abdu'l-Baha were men of different shades of thought, met to express their sympathy with the work and mission of their great visitor. Professor Michael E. Sadler was in the chair.

The meeting began with the Lord's Prayer spoken by the entire assembly; this was followed by the prayer for Unity of Baha'u'llah and a prayer of the fifth Century, ascribed to Pope Gelasius. Professor Sadler then spoke in words that will never be forgotten by those who heard them; and in his address used a quotation from a Universal Prayer, which had been submitted by an earnest Baha'i to Abdu'l-Baha, the year before in Egypt and which had been completed by him and commended as one that could be used by peoples of all faiths in the East and West.

The Chairman was followed by Sir Richard Stapley, Mr. Eric Hammond, Mr. Claude Montefiore, Mrs. Stannard from Egypt, and others. As Abdu'l-Baha left the hall, the poor people of the neighbourhood, crowded on the pavement to see him and an eager-faced little lame girl on crutches was specially brought to him.

Meeting of Farewell to Abdu'l-Baha.

Reprinted by kind permission, from the Christian Commonwealth of Oct. 4th.

September 29th, 1911.

AT the invitation of Mrs. Thornburgh-Cropper about four hundred and sixty representative people met in the hall of the Passmore Edwards' Settlement, Tavistock Place, last Friday evening to bid farewell to Abdu'l-Baha Abbas on the eve of his departure for Paris. Arriving in London on Monday evening, September the fourth, he has spent a happy and busy four weeks in our midst. Except for a brief visit to Bristol last week he remained at 97, Cadogan Gardens. His time was mainly occupied in interviews with people who wish to meet him. These included not a few whose names are household words in this country, and some travelled long distances to see him.

A beautiful spirit prevailed on Friday evening. The atmosphere was very different from that of an ordinary meeting or religious gathering. Everyone present was enriched by the lofty spiritual tone of the proceedings; the notes struck were all in the direction of Brotherhood, Unity, and Peace. While a report of the speeches would give a very inadequate idea of the effect produced, yet they were so well-conceived, so sincere, so exquisitely phrased as to be all worthy of reproduction. Among others Amir Ali Siyyid wrote regretting his inability to be present, and Archdeacon Wilberforce sent affectionate greetings.

After the Lord's Prayer and prayers for Unity of Baha'u'llah and Gelasius (fifth Century), Professor Michael Sadler spoke as follows:--

Speech of Professor Michael Sadler

We have met together to bid farewell to Abdu'l-Baha, and to thank God for his example and teaching, and for the power of his prayers to bring Light into confused thought, Hope into the place of dread, Faith where doubt was, and into troubled hearts, the Love which overmasters self-seeking and fear.

Though we all, among ourselves, in our devotional allegiance have our own individual loyalties, to all of us Abdu'l-Baha brings, and has brought, a message of Unity, of sympathy and of Peace. He bids us all be real and true in what we profess to believe; and to treasure above everything the Spirit behind the form. With him we bow before the Hidden Name, before that which is of every life the Inner Life! He bids us worship in fearless loyalty to our own faith, but with ever stronger yearning after Union, Brotherhood, and Love; so turning ourselves in Spirit, and with our whole heart, that we may enter more into the mind of God, which is above class, above race, and beyond time.

Professor Sadler concluded with a beautiful prayer of James Martineau.

Mr. Eric Hammond said the Baha'i movement stood for unity; one God, one people; a myriad souls manifesting the divine unity, a unity so complete that no difference of colour or creed could possibly differentiate between one Manifestation of God and another, and a sympathy so all-embracing as to include the very lowest, meanest, shabbiest of men; unity, sympathy, brotherhood, leading up to a concord universal. He concluded with a saying of Baha'u'llah, that the divine cause of universal good could not be limited to either East or West.

Miss Alice Buckton said we were standing at one of the springtimes of the world, and from that assembly of representatives of thought and work and love, would go out all over the world influences making for unity and brotherhood The complete equality of men and women was one of the chief notes of Baha'i teaching.

Sir Richard Stapley pointed out that unity must not be sought in the forms and externals of religion, but in the inner spirit. In Persia there had been such an impulse towards real unity as was a rebuke to this so-called Christian country.

Mr. Claude Montefiore, as a Jew, rejoiced in the growth of the spirit of unity, and regarded that meeting as prophetic of the better time to come, and in some sense a fulfillment of the idea expressed by one who fell as a martyr to the Roman Catholic faith, Sir Thomas More, who wrote of the great Church of the Utopians, in which all varieties of creeds gathered together, having a service and liturgy that expressed the higher unity, while admitting special loyalties.

Mrs. Stannard dwelt on what that meeting and the sentiments expressed meant to the East, especially to the women, whose condition it was difficult for the West to understand.

Tammaddun'ul-Mulk testified to the unifying effect the Baha'i movement had had in Persia, and of the wonderful way in which it had spread to America and other countries.

Then Abdu'l-Baha rose to give his farewell address. An impressive figure, the face rather worn but the eyes full of animation, he stood for about fifteen minutes, speaking in soft musical Persian. With hands extended, palms upwards, he closed with a prayer.

Farewell words of Abdu'l-Baha

O NOBLE friends and seekers for the Kingdom of God! About sixty years ago in the time when the fire of war was blazing among the nations of the world, and bloodshed was considered an honour to mankind; in a time when the carnage of thousands stained the earth; when children were rendered fatherless; when fathers were without sons and mothers were spent with weeping; when the darkness of inter-racial hatred and animosity seemed to envelope mankind and blot out the divine light; when the wafting of the holy breath of God seemed to be cut off--in that time Baha'u'llah rose like a shining star from the horizon of Persia, inspired with the message of Peace and of Brotherhood among men.

He brought the light of guidance to the world; He kindled the fire of love and revealed the great reality of the True Beloved. He sought to destroy the foundations of religious and racial prejudice and of political rivalry.

He likened the world of humanity to a tree, and all the nations to its branches and the people to its leaves, buds and fruits.

His mission was to change ignorant fanaticism into Universal love, to establish in the minds of His followers the basis of the unity of humanity and to bring about in practice the equality of mankind. He declared that all men were equal under the mercy and bounty of God.

Then was the door of the Kingdom set wide and the light of a new heaven on earth revealed unto seeing eyes.

Yet the whole Baha'u'llah's life was spent in the midst of great trial and cruel tyranny. In Persia He was thrown into prison, put into chains, and lived constantly under the menace of the sword. He was scorned and scourged.

When He was about thirty years old He was exiled to Baghdad, and from Baghdad to Constantinople, and from there to Adrianople and lastly to the prison of Akka.

Yet under chains and from His cell He succeeded in spreading His cause, and uplifting the banner of the oneness of humanity.

Now, God be praised, we see the light of Love shining in the East and in the West; and the tent of fellowship is raised in the midst of all the peoples for the drawing together of all hearts and souls.

The call of the Kingdom has been sounded, and the annunciation of the world's need for Universal Peace has enlightened the world's conscience.

My hope is that through the zeal and ardour of the pure of heart, the darkness of hatred and difference will be entirely abolished, and the light of love and unity shall shine; this world shall become a new world; things material shall become the mirror of the divine; human hearts shall meet and embrace each other; the whole world become as a man's native country and the different races be counted as one race.

Then disputes and differences will vanish, and the Divine Beloved be revealed on this earth.

As the East and the West are illumined by one sun, so all races, nations, and creeds shall be seen as the servants of the One God. The whole earth is one home, and all peoples, did they but know it, are bathed in the oneness of God's mercy. God created all. He gives sustenance to all. He guides and trains all under the shadow of his bounty. We must follow the example God Himself gives us, and do away with all disputations and quarrels.

Praise be to God! the signs of friendship are appearing, and as a proof of this I, today, coming from the East, have met in this London of the West with extreme kindness, regard and love, and I am deeply thankful and happy. I shall never forget this time I am spending with you.

Forty years I endured in a Turkish prison. Then in 1908 the Young Turks "Committee of Union and Progress" shook the gates of despotism and set all prisoners free, myself among them. I pray that blessing may be upon all who work for Union and Progress.

In the future untrue reports will be spread regarding Baha'u'llah in order to hinder the spread of Truth. I tell you this, that you may be awake and prepared.

I leave you with prayer that all the beauty of the Kingdom may be yours. In deep regret at our separation, I bid you good-bye.

The translation of the valedictory having been read by Professor Sadler, Abdu'l-Baha closed the meeting by giving his blessing in undulating rhythmic tones.

By the time these lines appear Abdu'l-Baha Abbas will have left our shores, but the memory of his gracious personality is a permanent possession. His influence will be felt for many days to come, and has already done much to promote that union of East and West for which many have long yearned.

10 Cheniston Gardens London W.

The subjoined notes are taken from "The Quarterly Record of `Higher Thought' Work," November 1911.

ONE of the most interesting and significant events which have taken place, has been the visit of Abdu'l-Baha to London. The Persian Mage whose life, passed in prison, has been spent in promoting peace and unity by the one certain method of aiding individual spiritual development, must in a very real sense have "tasted of the travail of his soul and been satisfied". Not only was he visited privately by nearly every earnest truth-seeker and leader of high thought in London, but his message was made known to thousands who had but dimly heard his name before.

The Higher Thought Centre was well known to Abdu'l-Baha as the place where the Baha'is held their weekly meetings under the direction of Miss Rosenberg, and an invitation to the Centre was accepted by him just two days before his departure. Through his interpreter Abdu'l-Baha gave a kindly greeting and a short impressive address, dwelling on the blessedness of such an assembly gathered in a spirit of unity and spiritual aspiration. He concluded with a lowly uttered fervent prayer in his own tongue, and a benediction which all present felt to be very real.

On the following day a message was conveyed to the Centre from Abdu'l-Baha signifying the fullest appreciation of all kindness shown to the Baha'is, and concluding with these words; "it matters not what name each calls himself--The Great Work is One."

"Christ is ever in the world of existence. He has never disappeared out of it.... Rest assured that Christ is present. The Spiritual beauty we see around us today is from the breathings of Christ."

A Message from Abdu'l-Baha Written for The Christian Commonwealth and published

September 29th, 1911.

GOD sends Prophets for the education of the people and the progress of mankind. Each such Manifestation of God has raised humanity. They serve the whole world by the bounty of God. The sure proof that they are the Manifestations of God is in the education and progress of the people. The Jews were in the lowest condition of ignorance, and captives under Pharaoh when Moses appeared and raised them to a high state of civilization. Thus was the reign of Solomon brought about and science and art were made known to mankind. Even Greek philosophers became students of Solomon's teaching. Thus was Moses proved to be a Prophet.

After the lapse of time the Israelites deteriorated, and became subject to the Romans and the Greeks. Then the brilliant Star of Jesus rose from the horizon upon the Israelites, brightening the world, until all sects and creeds and nations were taught the beauty of unity. There cannot be any better proof than this that Jesus was the Word of God.

So it was with the Arabian nations who, being uncivilized, were oppressed by the Persian and Greek governments. When the Light of Muhammad shone forth all Arabia was brightened. These oppressed and degraded peoples became enlightened and cultured; so much so, indeed, that other nations imbibed Arabian civilization from Arabia. This was the proof of Muhammad's divine mission.

All the teaching of the Prophets is one; one faith; one Divine light shining throughout the world. Now, under the banner of the oneness of humanity all people of all creeds should turn away from prejudice and become friends and believers in all the Prophets. As Christians believe in Moses, so the Jews should believe in Jesus. As the Muhammadans believe in Christ and Moses, so likewise the Jews and the Christians should believe in Muhammad. Then all disputes would disappear, all then would be united. Baha'u'llah came for this purpose. He has made the three religions one. He has uplifted the standard of the oneness of faith and the honour of humanity in the centre of the world. Today we must gather round it, and try with heart and soul to bring about the union of mankind. Discourse given at Miss E. J. Rosenberg's

Unity Meeting.

September 8th, 1911.

PRAISE be to God, that such a meeting of purity and steadfastness is being held in London. The hearts of those present are pure, and are turned towards the Kingdom of God. I hope that all that is contained and established in the Holy books of God may be realized in you. The Messengers of God are the principal and the first teachers. Whenever this world becomes dark, and divided in its opinions and indifferent, God will send one of His Holy Messengers.

Moses came during a time of darkness, when ignorance and childishness prevailed amongst the people, and they were waverers. Moses was the teacher of God; He gave the teachings of holiness and educated the Israelites. He raised up the people from their degradation and caused them to be highly honoured. He taught them Sciences and Arts, trained them in civilization and increased their human virtues. After a while, that which they had thus received from God was lost; the way was prepared for the return of evil qualities, and the world was oppressed by tyranny.

Then again the rumour of the Light of Reality and the breathing of the Holy Spirit became known. The cloud of Bounty showered, the Light of Guidance shone upon the earth. The world put on a new garment, the people became a new people, the oneness of humanity was proclaimed. The great unity of thought transformed humanity and created a new world. Again, after a time, all this was forgotten by the people. The teachings of God no longer influenced their lives. His prophecies and commandments became fainter and were finally obliterated from their hearts, and tyranny and thoughtlessness once more prevailed.

Baha'u'llah then came and once more renewed the foundation of Faith. He brought back the teachings of God, and the humane practices of the time of Christ. He quenched the thirst of the thirsty, He awakened the careless and called the attention of the heedless to the Divine secrets. He declared the unity of humanity, and spread abroad the teaching of the equality of all men.

Therefore, all of you ought with your hearts and minds to endeavour to win the people with kindness, so that this great Unity may be established, that childish superstitions may pass away, and all may become one.

Discourse at Mrs. Thornburgh-Cropper's

September 13th, 1911.

ABDU'L-BAHA said:--Thanks be to God, this is a good meeting. It is very enlightened, it is spiritual.

As a Persian Poet has written:--"The Celestial Universe is so formed that the under world reflects the upper world." That is to say whatever exists in heaven is reflected in this phenomenal world. Now, praise be to God, this meeting of ours is a reflection of the heavenly concourse; it is as though we had taken a mirror and had gazed into it. This reflection from the heavenly concourse we know as love.

As heavenly love exists in the supreme concourse even so it is reflected here. The supreme concourse is filled with the desire for God--thank God, this desire is also here.

Therefore if we say that this meeting is heavenly, it is true. Why? Because we have no other desire except for that which comes from God. We have no other object save the commemoration of God.

Some of the people of the earth desire conquest over others: some of them are longing for rest and ease; others desire a high position; some desire to become famous:--thank God our desire is for spirituality and for union with God.

Now that we are gathered here our wish is to raise the banner of the Unity of God, to spread the Light of God, to make the hearts of the people turn to the Kingdom. Therefore I thank God that He is causing us to do this great work.

I pray for all of you, that you may become celestial warriors, that you may everywhere spread the Unity of God and enlighten the East and West, and that you may give to all hearts the love of God. This is my utmost desire, and I pray to God that your desire may be the same.

I am very happy to be with you all. I am pleased with the English King and Government, and with the people.

You may thank God that in this land you are so free. You do not know what lack of freedom there is in the East. When anyone comes to this country he is content.

I wish God's protection for you all. Goodbye to you all.

Discourse by Abdu'l-Baha given at the

Unity Meeting of Misses Jack and Herrick.

September 22nd, 1911.

IT is a cold and miserable day but as I was anxious to see you I came here. For a man who has love, effort is a rest. He will travel any distance to visit his friends.

Thank God I see you spiritual and at rest; I give you this message from God; that you must be turned toward Him. Praise God that you are near Him! The unworthy things of this world have not deterred you from seeking the world of Spirit. When in harmony with that world, you care not for the things that perish; your desire is for that which never dies and the Kingdom lies open before you. I hope that the teaching of God will spread throughout the world, and will cause all to be united.

In the time of Jesus Christ there was an outpouring of the Light from East to West that brought the people under a heavenly banner and illumined them with divine insight. Western lands have been kindled by the Light of the Christ. I pray earnestly that the Light in this advanced age will so illumine the world that all may rally under the banner of Unity and receive Spiritual education.

Then those problems which cause difference among the peoples of the earth will be seen no more, for verily they are not. You are all waves of one sea, mirrors of one reflection.

This day the countries of Europe are at rest; Education has become widespread. The light of liberty is the light of the West, and the intention of government is to work for truth and justice in Western countries. But ever the light of spirituality shines from out of the East. In this age that light has become dimmed; religion has become a matter of form and ceremony and the desire for God's love has been lost.

In very age of great spiritual darkness, a light is kindled in the East. So once again the light of the teachings of God has come unto you. Even as education and progress travel from West to East, so does the spiritual fire travel from East to West.

I hope that the people of the West may be illumined by the light of God; that the Kingdom may come to them, that they may find eternal Life, that the Spirit of God may spread like a fire among them, that they may be baptized with the Water of Life and may find a new birth.

This is my desire; I hope by the will of God, He will cause you to receive it, and will make you happy.

In the same way that you have education and material progress so may the light of God be your portion.

God keep all of you in safety.

Notes of Conversations

The Arrival in London

THE evening of his arrival in London, Monday, September 4th, 1911, Abdu'l-Baha said: Heaven has blessed this day. It was said that London should be a place for a great proclamation of the Faith. I was tired when I went on board the steamer, but when I reached London and beheld the faces of the friends my fatigue left me. Your great love refreshes me. I am very pleased with the English friends.

The feeling that existed between the East and the West is changing in the Light of Baha'u'llah's teaching. It used to be such that if an Occidental drank from the cup of an Oriental the cup would be considered polluted and would be broken. Now when a Western Baha'i dines with an Eastern Baha'i the vessels and the plates that he has used are kept apart and reverenced in his memory. Abdu'l-Baha then gave this historic instance of wonderful brotherly love:

One day some soldiers came to the house of a Baha'i and demanded that one of the guests should be given up for execution, according to their warrant. The host took his guest's place and died in his stead.

London

The magnet of your love brought me to this country. My hope is that the Divine Light may shine here, and that the Heavenly Star of Baha'u'llah may strengthen you, so that you may be the cause of the oneness of humanity, that you may help to make the darkness of superstition and prejudice disappear and unite all creeds and nations.

This is a brilliant century. Eyes are now open to the beauty of the oneness of humanity, of love and of brotherhood. The darkness of suppression will disappear and the light of unity will shine. We cannot bring love and unity to pass merely by talking of it. Knowledge is not enough. Wealth, science, education are good, we know: but we must also work and study to bring to maturity the fruit of knowledge.

Knowledge is the first step; resolve, the second step; action, its fulfillment, is the third step. To construct a building one must first of all make a plan, then one must have the power (money), then one can build. A society of Unity is formed, that is good-- but meetings and discussions are not enough. In Egypt these meetings take place but there is only talk and no result. These meetings here in London are good, the knowledge and the intention are good, but how can there be a result without action? Today the force for Unity is the Holy Spirit of Baha'u'llah. He manifested this spirit of Unity. Baha'u'llah brings East and West together. Go back, search history, you will not find a precedent for this.

Differences

God has created the world as one--the boundaries are marked out by man. God has not divided the lands, but each man has his house and meadow; horses and dogs do not divide the fields into parts. That is why Baha'u'llah says: "Let not a man glory in that he loves his country, but that he loves his kind." All are of one family, one race; all are human beings. Differences as to the partition of lands should not be the cause of separation among the people.

One of the great reasons of separation is colour. Look how this prejudice has power in America, for instance. See how they hate one another! Animals do not quarrel because of their colour! Surely man who is so much higher in creation, should not be lower than the animals. Think over this. What ignorance exists! White doves do not quarrel with blue doves because of their colour, but white men fight with dark-coloured men. This racial prejudice is the worst of all.

The Old Testament says that God created man like unto His own image; in the Qur'an it says: "There is no difference in the Creation of God!" Think well, God has created all, cares for all, and all are under His protection. The policy of God is better than our policy. We are not as wise as God!

Religion

To most men who have not heard the message of this teaching, religion seems an outward form, a pretence, merely a seal of respectability. Some priests are in holy office for no other reason than to gain their living. They themselves do not believe in the religion they pretend to teach. Would these men lay down their lives for their faith? Ask a Christian of this kind to deny Christ in order to save his life, and he will do it.

Ask a Baha'i to deny any of the great Prophets, to deny his faith or to deny Moses, Muhammad or Christ, and he will say: I would rather die. So a Muhammadan Baha'i is a better Christian than many so called Christians.

A Baha'i denies no religion; he accepts the Truth in all, and would die to uphold it. He loves all men as his brothers, of whatever class, of whatever race or nationality, of whatever creed or colour, whether good or bad, rich or poor, beautiful or hideous. He commits no violence; if he is struck he does not return the blow. He calls nothing bad, following the example of the Lord Baha'u'llah. As a safeguard against intemperance he does not drink wine or spirits. Baha'u'llah has said it is not good for a sane man to take that which will destroy his health and sense.

The religion of God has two aspects in this world. The spiritual (the real) and the formal (the outward). The formal side changes, as man changes from age to age. The spiritual side which is the Truth, never changes. The Prophets and Manifestations of God bring always the same teaching; at first men cling to the Truth but after a time they disfigure it. The Truth is distorted by man-made outward forms and material laws. The veil of substance and worldliness is drawn across the reality of Truth.

As Moses and Jesus brought their Message to the people, so Baha'u'llah brings the same Message.

Each time God sends a Great One to us we are given new life, but the Truth each Manifestation brings is the same. The Truth never changes but man's vision changes. It is dulled and confused by the complication of outward forms.

The Truth is easy to understand although the outward forms in which it is expressed bewilder the intelligence. As men grow they see the futility of man-made forms and despise them. Therefore many leave the churches, because the latter often emphasize the external only.

Discourse to an assembly of Theosophists.

London - September, 1911.

THESE are wonderful days! We see an Eastern guest received with love and courtesy in the West. I have been drawn here, in spite of indisposition, by the magnet of your love and sympathy.

Some years ago an Ambassador was sent from Persia to London where he stayed five years. (His name was Abdu'l Hasan Khan). When he returned to Persia they asked him to tell them about the English people. He answered: "I do not know the English people, although I have been in London for years I have only met the people of the Court." This man was a great man in Persia, and was sent to England by princes, and yet he did not know the people, although he had lived among them five years. Now, I--long a prisoner, come to England for the first time, and although my visit is so short, I have already met many dear friends, and I can say I know the people. Those I have met are true souls working for peace and unity.--Think what a difference there is between this time we are living in now, and seventy years ago! Think of the progress! the progress towards unity and peace.

It is God's will that the differences between nations should disappear. Those who help on the cause of unity are doing God's work. Unity is the Divine Bounty for this luminous century. Praise be to God, there are today many societies and many meetings held for Unity. Enmity is not so much the cause of separation as it used to be; the cause of disunion now is mostly prejudice. For instance, years ago when Europeans visited the East they were considered unclean and were hated. Now it is different: when people of the West visit those in the East who are followers of the New Light, they are received with love and courtesy.

Abdu'l-Baha holding a little child close to him said, the true Baha'i loves the children, because Jesus says they are of the Kingdom of heaven. A simple pure heart is near to God; a child has no worldly ambitions.

Prejudices

The Universal Races Congress was good, for it was intended for the furtherance and progress of unity among all nations and a better international understanding. The purpose was good. The causes of dispute among different nations are always due to one of the following classes of prejudice: racial, lingual, theological, personal, and prejudices of custom and tradition. It requires a universal active force to overcome these differences. A small disease needs a small remedy, but a disease which pervades the whole body needs a very strong remedy. A small lamp may light a room, a larger would light a house, a larger still might shine through the city, but the sun is needed to light the whole world.

The differences in language cause disunion between nations. There must be one universal language. The diversity in Faiths is also a cause of separation. The true foundation of all faiths must be established, the outer differences abolished. There must be a Oneness of Faith. To end all these differences is a very hard task. The whole world is sick, and needs the power of the Great Healer.

These meetings teach us that Unity is good, and that suppression (slavery under the yoke of tradition and prejudice) is the cause of disunion. To know this is not enough. All knowledge is good, but it can bear no fruit except by action. It is well to know that riches are good, but that knowledge will not make a man rich; he must work, he must put his knowledge into practice. We hope the people realize and know that unity is good, and we also hope that they will not be content to stand still in that knowledge. Do not only say that Unity, Love and Brotherhood are good; you must work for their realization.

The Czar of Russia suggested the Hague Peace Conference and proposed a decrease in armament for all nations. In this Conference it was proved that Peace was beneficial to all countries, and that war destroyed trade, etc. The Czar's words were admirable though after the conference was over he himself was the first to declare war (against Japan).

Knowledge is not enough; we hope by the Love of God we shall put it into practice. A spiritual universal Force is needed for this. Meetings are good for engendering spiritual force. To know that it is possible to reach a state of perfection, is good; to march forward on the path is better. We know that to help the poor and to be merciful is good and pleases God, but knowledge alone does not feed the starving man, nor can the poor be warmed by knowledge or words in the bitter winter; we must give the practical help of Loving-kindness.

What of the Peace Congress?

It resembles many drunkards gathered together to protest against the drinking of alcohol. They say drink is horrible and they straightway go out from the house to drink again.

Theosophy

When Abdu'l-Baha was asked if he recognized the good which the Theosophical Society has done. He replied:

I know it; I think a great deal of it. I know that their desire is to serve mankind. I thank this noble Society in the name of all Baha'is and for myself. I hope that by God's help these friends will succeed in bringing about love and unity. It is a great work and needs the effort of all the servants of God!

Peace

During the last six thousand years nations have hated one another, it is now time to stop. War must cease. Let us be united and love one another and await the result. We know the effects of war are bad. So let us try, as an experiment, peace, and if the results of peace are bad, then we can choose if it would be better to go back to the old state of war! Let us in any case make the experiment. If we see that unity brings Light we shall continue it. For six thousand years we have been walking on the left-hand path; let us walk on the right-hand path now. We have passed many centuries in darkness, let us advance towards the light.

Question.--(It was remarked, Theosophy teaches that truth in all the religions is the same): Does the task of unifying all religions have Abdu'l-Baha's sympathy?

Answer.--Surely.

Question.--Can Abdu'l-Baha suggest any lines on which it could best be worked out?

Answer.--Search for truth. Seek the realities in all religions. Put aside all superstitions. Many of us do not realize the Reality of all Religions.

Divine Manifestations

Question.--What is Abdu'l-Baha's teaching concerning the different Divine manifestations?

Answer.--The Reality of all is One. Truth is one. Religions are like the branches of one Tree. One branch is high, one is low and one in the centre, yet all draw their life from the one stem. One branch bears fruit and others are not laden so abundantly. All the Prophets are lights, they only differ in degree; they shine like brilliant heavenly bodies, each have their appointed place and time of ascension. Some are like lamps, some like the moon, some like distant stars, and a few are like the sun, shining from one end of the earth to the other. all have the same Light to give, yet they are different in degree.

Buddhism

Some referred to the teaching of Buddha. Abdu'l-Baha said: The real teaching of Buddha is the same as the teaching of Jesus Christ. The teachings of all the Prophets are the same in character. Now men have changed the teaching. If you look at the present practice of the Buddhist religion, you will see that there is little of the Reality left. Many worship idols although their teaching forbids it.

Buddha had disciples and he wished to send them out into the world to teach, so he asked them questions to see if they were prepared as he would have them be. "When you go to the East and to the West," said the Buddha, "and the people shut their doors to you and refuse to speak to you, what will you do?"--The disciples answered and said: "We shall be very thankful that they do us no harm."--"Then if they do you harm and mock, what will you do?"--"We shall be very thankful that they do not give us worse treatment."--"If they throw you into prison?"--"We shall still be grateful that they do not kill us."--"What if they were to kill you?" the Master asked for the last time. "Still," answered the disciples, "we will be thankful, for they cause us to be martyrs. What more glorious fate is there than this, to die for the glory of God?" And the Buddha said: "Well done!"

The teaching of Buddha was like a young and beautiful child, and now it has become as an old and decrepit man. Like the aged man it cannot see, it cannot hear, it cannot remember anything. Why go so far back? Consider the laws of the Old Testament: the Jews do not follow Moses as their example nor keep his commands. So it is with many other religions.

How can we get the power to follow the right path?

By putting the teaching into practice power will be given. You know which path to follow: you cannot be mistaken, for there's a great distinction between God and evil, between Light and darkness, Truth and falsehood, Love and hatred, Generosity and meanness, Education and ignorance, Faith in God and superstition, good Laws and unjust laws.

Faith

How can one increase in faith?

You must strive. A child does not know, in learning he obtains knowledge. search for Truth.

There are three kinds of Faith: first, that which is from tradition and birth. For example: a child is born of Muhammadan parents, he is a Muhammadan. This faith is weak traditional faith: second, that which comes from Knowledge, and is the faith of understanding. This is good, but there is a better, the faith of practice. This is real faith.

We hear there is an invention, we believe it is good; then we come and see it. We hear that there is wealth, we see it; we work hard for it, and become rich ourselves and so help others. We know and we see the Light, we go close to it, are warmed by it, and reflect its rays on others; this is real faith, and thus we receive power to become the eternal sons of God.

Healing

Abdu'l-Baha said: Disease is of two kinds: material and spiritual.

Take for instance, a cut hand; if you pray for the cut to be healed and do not stop its bleeding, you will not do much good; a material remedy is needed.

Sometimes if the nervous system is paralyzed through fear, a spiritual remedy is necessary. Madness, incurable otherwise,. can be cured through prayer. It often happens that sorrow makes one ill, this can be cured by spiritual means.

Philanthropic Societies

Someone asked if the Humanitarian Society was good.--Yes all societies, all organizations, working for the betterment of the human race are good, very good. All who work for their brothers and sisters have Baha'u'llah's blessing. They will surely succeed.

Abdu'l-Baha said: It makes me happy to see all the believers in London. You are all, of every race and creed, members of one family. The teaching of Baha'u'llah constrains you to realize your brotherhood to one another.

Man's Comprehension of God and of Higher Worlds

To man, the Essence of God is incomprehensible, so also are the worlds beyond this, and their condition. It is given to man to obtain knowledge, to attain to great spiritual perfection, to discover hidden truths and to manifest even the attributes of God; but still man cannot comprehend the Essence of God. Where the ever-widening circle of man's knowledge meets the spiritual world a Manifestation of God is sent to mirror forth His splendour.

Divine Manifestations

Is the Divine Manifestation, God?

Yes, and yet not in Essence. A Divine Manifestation is as a mirror reflecting the light of the Sun. The light is the same and yet the mirror is not the Sun. All the Manifestations of God bring the same Light; they only differ in degree, not in reality. The Truth is one. The light is the same though the lamps may be different; we must look at the Light not at the Lamp. If we accept the Light in one, we must accept the Light in all; all agree, because all are the same. The teaching is ever the same, it is only the outward forms that change.

The Manifestations of God are as the heavenly bodies. All have their appointed place and time of ascension, but the Light they give is the same. if one wishes to look for the sun rising, one does not look always at the same point because that point changes with the seasons. When one sees the sun rise further in the north one recognizes it, though it has risen at a different point.

Notes of a conversation with Abdu'l-Baha

A COLOURED man from South Africa who was visiting Abdu'l-Baha, said that even now no white people really cared very much for the black man.

Abdu'l-Baha replies: Compare the present time and the feeling towards the coloured people now, with the state of feeling two or three hundred years ago, and see how much better it is at present. In a short time the relationship between the coloured and white people will still further improve, and bye and bye no difference will be felt between them. White doves and purple doves exist, but both kinds are doves.

Baha'u'llah once compared the coloured people to the black pupil of the eye surrounded by the white. In this black pupil you see the reflection of that which is before it, and through it the light of the Spirit shines forth.

In the sight of God colour makes no difference at all, He looks at the hearts of men. That which God desires from men is the heart. A black man with a good character is far superior to a white man with a character that is less good.

Ideals of East and West

One of the organizers of the Races Congress present spoke of the Western ideals of Baha'u'llah as differing from those of former prophets which were tinged with the ideas and civilization of the East. He then asked whether Baha'u'llah had made a special study of Western writings, and founded his teachings in accordance with them.

Abdu'l-Baha laughed heartily, and said that the books of Baha'u'llah, written and printed sixty years ago, contained the ideals now so familiar to the West, but, at that time, they had not been printed or thought of in the West. Besides, he continued, supposing that a very advanced thinker from the West had gone to visit Baha'u'llah and to teach Him, would the name of such a great man and the fact of his visit have been unknown and unrecorded? No! In former days, in the time of the Buddha and Zoroaster, civilization in Asia and in the East was very much higher than in the West and ideas and thoughts of the Eastern peoples were much in advance of, and nearer to the thoughts of God than those of the West. But since that time superstitions had crept into the religion and ideals of the East, and from many differing causes the ideals and characters of the Eastern peoples had gone down and down, lower and lower, while the Western peoples had been constantly advancing and struggling towards the Light. Consequently, in these days, the civilization of the West was much higher than that of the East, and the ideas and thoughts of the people of the West were much nearer to the thought of God than those of the East. Therefore, the ideals of Baha'u'llah had been more quickly realized in the West.

Abdu'l-Baha showed further how Baha'u'llah had exactly described in one of his books what has since been carried out in the International Council of Arbitration, describing its various functions, some of which have not yet been realized and he (Abdu'l-Baha) would describe them to us now, so that when they were fulfilled, as they would be in the near future, we might know that they had been prophesied by Baha'u'llah.

War was the greatest calamity that could overtake the nations, because the people usually employed in agriculture, trades, commerce, and other useful arts, were taken away from their various occupations and turned into soldiers, so that there was great waste and loss, in addition to the destruction and carnage of war.

Baha'u'llah had said that the functions of the International Court would be to settle disputes that arose from time to time between the nations; to define the exact boundaries of the different countries, and to decide what number of soldiers and guns should be maintained by each nation, according to its population, in order to preserve internal order. For instance, one country might have ten thousand soldiers, another twenty thousand, another fifteen thousand, and so on, in accordance with the size and population of the nation; also if any people rebelled against the decision of the Court and rejected it, the Court would empower the others to join their forces and to endorse their decision, if need be, by united action.

We had not seen any of these things actualized as yet, but we should do so in the future.

Science and Faith

The gentleman then put a question which he said he considered of very great importance in connection with a religious movement, claiming to be universal. What position he asked, if any, did Baha'u'llah given to the modern ideas and conceptions of Science in his teachings. The whole structure of modern civilization is based upon the results and the knowledge obtained through laborious and patient observation of facts collected by men of Science: in some cases through hundreds of years of painstaking investigation. To make his meaning clearer, he instanced the ethic, and the moral teachings of the Chinese philosophers, than which he could conceive nothing higher. However, these teachings had very little effect outside of China, for the reason he considered, that they were not primarily based on the teachings of Science.

Abdu'l-Baha replied that a very great importance was given to Science and knowledge in the writings of Baha'u'llah, who wrote that, if a man educated the children of the poor, who could not themselves afford to do so, it was, in the sight of God, as if he had educated the Son of God.

If any religion rejected Science and knowledge, that religion was false. Science and Religion should go forward together; indeed, they should be like two fingers of one hand.

Baha'u'llah had also in His writings given a most important place to Art, and the practice of skilled trades. He had stated that the practice of an Art or Trade in the true spirit of service was identical with the worship of God.

A gentleman connected with the work of a Settlement then asked what was the best method of raising up and civilizing the very lowest and most degraded and ignorant of the people and would their education come about gradually through the enlightenment of the Spirit, or was there any special means we could adopt to further this end?

Abdu'l-Baha replied that the best way was to give them spiritual teachings and enlightenment. He also remarked that the way to broaden the outlook of the very narrow-hearted and prejudiced, and to make them listen to a wider teaching, was by showing towards them the greatest kindness and love. The example of our lives was of more value than words.

Converse with Departed Persons

The question was asked if it were possible to establish communication with the dead, and whether it was wise or advisable to attend seances or to engage in table-turning, spirit-rapping, etc.

The Master said these rappings, etc., were all material things, and of the body. What is needed is to rise above the material to the realms of the purely Spiritual. Table-turning and such like were material, a natural result, and not spiritual.

But it was possible to communicate with the dead through the condition of the character and the heart.

Are Superstitions Useful

A lady enquired whether some superstitions might not be good for ignorant people, who, if they were without them might perhaps be without beliefs of any kind?

Abdu'l-Baha replied that superstitions were of two kinds; those that were harmful and dangerous, and those that were harmless and produced certain good effects.

For example, there were some poor people who believed that misfortunes and punishments were caused by a Great Angel with a sword in his hand, who struck down those who stole, and committed murder and crimes.

They thought the flashes of lightning were the weapons of this angel, and that if they did wrong they would be struck by lightning. This belief caused them to refrain from evil actions.

The Chinese held a superstition that if they burn certain pieces of paper this will drive the devils away; they sometimes burnt these pieces of paper on board ships when they were travelling in order to drive away devils, and by so doing they set fire to the ships and destroyed many lives. This was a type of dangerous and harmful superstition.

The Life After Death

Mrs. S. asked some questions with reference to the conditions of existence in the next world, and the life after death; she said that having recently lost a very near relative, she had given much thought to this subject. Many thought that re-union with those we had loved, and who had passed on to the future life, would only take place after a long period of time had elapsed. She wished to know whether one would be re-united with those who had gone before immediately after death.

Abdu'l-Baha answered that this would depend upon the respective stations of the two. If both had the same degree of development, they would be re-united immediately after death. The questioner then said, how could this state of development be acquired? Abdu'l-Baha replied, by unceasing effort, striving to do right, and to attain spiritual qualities.

The questioner remarked that many differing opinions were held as to the conditions of the future life. Some thought that all would have exactly the same perfections and virtues; that all would be equal and alike.

Abdu'l-Baha said there would be variety, and differing degrees of attainment, as in this world.

The question was then asked as to how it would be possible with no material bodies or environment to recognize different entities and characters, when all would be in the same conditions and on the same plane of existence.

Abdu'l-Baha said if several people look into a mirror at the same moment, they behold all the different personalities, their characteristics and movements; the glass of the mirror into which they look is one. In your mind you have a variety of thoughts, but all these thoughts are separate and distinct. Also you may perhaps have hundreds of friends; but when you call them before your memory you do not confuse them one with another: each one is separate and distinct, having their own individualities and characteristics.

Replying to another questioner, he said that when two people, husband and wife for instance, have been completely united in this life their souls being as one soul, then after one of them has passed away, this union of heart and soul would remain unbroken.

Spiritual Relationship

In the evening of September 28th, Abdu'l-Baha was with a number of assembled guests.

He said all of you here are sisters. Bodily relationships may pass; even two sisters may be inimical to each other, but the spiritual relationship is eternal, and brings about mutual love and service.

Be always kind to everyone and a refuge for

those who are without shelter.

Be daughters to those who are older than you.

Be sisters to those who are of your own age.

Be mothers to those who are younger than

yourselves.

Be nurses to the sick, treasurers for the poor,

and supply heavenly food to the hungry.

A Persian doctor from Qazvin said this was a great work of God that the East and the West had become so united, and we must always thank God that the Baha'i cause had produced such great harmony and union between us. The result of this visit of Abdu'l-Baha to the West would be very great.

A Baha'i Wedding

QUITE an oriental note was struck toward the end of Abdu'l-Baha's London visit, by the marriage of a young Persian couple who had sought his presence for the ceremony, the bride journeying from Baghdad accompanied by her uncle in order to meet her fiance here and be married before Abdu'l-Baha's departure. The bride's father and grandfather had been followers of Baha'u'llah during the time of his banishment.

We hesitate to alter the bridegroom's description of the service and therefore print it in his own simple and beautiful language. It will serve to show a side not touched on elsewhere, and without which no idea of his visit is complete. We refer to the attitude of reverence with which people from the East who came to see Abdu'l-Baha regard their great teacher. They invariably rise and stand with bowed heads whenever he enters the room.

Mirza Dawud writes:--

On Sunday morning, the 1st of October, 1911, A.D., equal to the 9th Tishi 5972 (Hebrew Era), Regina Nur Mahal Khanum, and Mirza Yuhanna Dawud were admitted into the holy presence of Abdu'l-Baha: may my life be a sacrifice to Him!

After receiving us, Abdu'l-Baha said, "You are very welcome and it makes me happy to see you here in London."

Looking at me he said, "Never have I united anyone in marriage before, except my own daughters, but as I love you much, and you have rendered a great service to the Kingdom of Abha, both in this country and in other lands, I will perform your marriage ceremony today. It is my hope that you may both continue in the blessed path of service."

Then, first, Abdu'l-Baha took Nur Mahal Khanum into the next room and said to her, "Do you love Mirza Yuhanna Dawud with all your heart and soul?" She answered, "Yes, I do."

Then Abdu'l-Baha called me to him and put a similar question, that is to say, "Do you love Nur Mahal Khanum with all your heart and soul?" I answered "Yes, I do." We re-entered the room together and Abdu'l-Baha took the right hand of the bride and gave it into that of the bridegroom and asked us to say after him, "We do all to please God."

We all sat down and Abdu'l-Baha continued; "Marriage is a holy institution and much encouraged in this blessed cause. Now you two are no longer two, but one. Baha'u'llah's wish is that all men be of one mind and consider themselves of one great household, that the mind of mankind be not divided against itself.

"It is my wish and hope that you may be blessed in your life. May God help you to render great service to the kingdom of Abha and may you become a means of its advancement.

"May joy be increased to you as the years go by, and may you become thriving trees bearing delicious and fragrant fruits which are the blessings in the path of service."

When we came out, all the assembled friends both of Persia and London congratulated us on the great honour that had been bestowed upon us, and we were invited to dine by the kind hostess.

After a little while we gathered around the table with him. During the meal one of the friends asked Abdu'l-Baha how he enjoyed his stay in London, and what he thought of the English people. I acted as interpreter. Abdu'l-Baha replied: "I have enjoyed London very much and the bright faces of the friends have delighted my heart. I was drawn here by their unity and love. In the world of existence there is no more powerful magnet than the magnet of love. These few days will pass away, but their import shall be remembered by God's friends in all ages and in all lands.

There are living nations and dead nations. Syria lost its civilization through lethargy of spirit. The English nation is a living one, and when in this spiritual springtime the divine truth come forth with renewed vitality, the English will be like fruitful trees, and the Holy Spirit will enable them to flourish in abundance. Then will they gain not only materially, but in that which is far more important, spiritual progress, which will enable them to render a greater service to the world of humanity."

Another asked why the teachings of all religions are expressed largely by parables and metaphors and not in the plain language of the people.

Abdu'l-Baha replied:--"Divine things are too deep to be expressed by common words. The heavenly teachings are expressed in parable in order to be understood and preserved for ages to come. When the spiritually minded dive deeply into the ocean of their meaning they bring to the surface the pearls of their inner significance. There is no greater pleasure than to study God's Word with a spiritual mind."

"The object of God's teaching to man is that man may know himself in order to comprehend the greatness of God. The Word of God is for agreement and concord. If you go to Persia where the friends of Abha are many, you will at once realize the unifying force of God's work. They are doing their utmost to strengthen this bond of amity. There, people of different nationalities gather in one meeting and chant the divine tablets with one accord. It might be supposed that they were all brethren. We do not consider anyone a stranger, for it is said by Baha'u'llah 'Ye are all the rays of one sun; the fruits of one tree; and the leaves of one branch.' We desire the true brotherhood of humanity. This shall be so, and it has already begun. Praise to be God, the Helper, the Pardoner!"

The visit to Bristol

ABDU'L-BAHA spent the week end of September 23rd to 25th, at the Clifton Guest House at Clifton, Bristol.

On the first afternoon, while driving, he expressed much interest in rural England, marvelling at the century-old trees, and the vivid green of the woods and downs, so unlike the arid East. "Though it is autumn it seems like spring," he said. The houses with their little plots of ground, suggested a quotation which Abdu'l-Baha gave from Baha'u'llah's writings in which the latter alludes to each family having a house with a piece of land. Abdu'l-Baha likened the country to the soul and the city to the body of man, saying, "The body without the soul cannot live. It is good," he remarked, "to live under the sky, in the sunshine and fresh air." Observing a young woman who rode by on horseback with her hair flying free and several who bicycled past on their bicycles unattended, he said, "This is the age of woman. She should receive the same education as her brother and enjoy the same privilege; for all souls are equal before God. Sex, in its relation to the exigencies of the physical plane, has no connection with the Spirit. In this age of spiritual awakening, the world has entered upon the path of progress into the arena of development, where the power of the spirit surpasses that of the body. Soon the spirit will have dominion over the world of humanity."

In the evening greetings were cabled to the Baha'is of Tihran informing them of Abdu'l-Baha's presence in Bristol. He sent his love and wished them to know that he was well and happy with the Clifton friends. This was sent in reply to a cablegram previously received from Tihran congratulating the people of the Guest House on his prospective visit.

Later on a general reception was held, ninety people coming to meet Abdu'l-Baha who spoke to them with impressive earnestness.

Abdu'l-Baha said, "You are very welcome. I have come far to see you. I praise God that after forty years of waiting I am permitted at last to come and bring my message. This is an assembly full of spirituality. Those who are present have turned their hearts towards God. They are looking and longing for glad tidings. We have gathered here by the power of the Spirit, therefore our hearts are stirred with thanksgiving. `Send out Thy Light and Thy Truth O God: Let them lead us to the Holy Mountains!' May we be refreshed by the holy springs that are renewing the life of the world! As day follows night, and after sunset comes the dawn, so Jesus Christ appeared on the horizon of this world like a Sun of Truth; even so when the people--after forgetting the teachings of Christ and His example of love to all humanity--had again grown tired of material things, a heavenly Star shone once more in Persia, a new illumination appeared and now a great light is spreading throughout all lands.

"Men keep their possessions for their own enjoyment and do not share sufficiently with others the bounty received from God. Spring is thus changed into the winter of selfishness and egotism. Jesus Christ said `Ye must be born again' so that divine Life may spring anew within you. Be kind to all around and serve one another; love to be just and true in all your dealings; pray always and so live your life that sorrow cannot touch you. Look upon the people of your own race and those of other races as members of one organism; sons of the same Father; let it be known by your behaviour that you are indeed the people of God. Then wars and disputes shall cease and over the world will spread the Most Great Peace."

After Abdu'l-Baha had retired Tamaddun'ul-Mulk and Mr. W. Tudor Pole gave short addresses in which references were made to the martyrdom of the faithful in Persia, special mention being made of the eminent poetess Qurratu'l-'Ayn.

The next day was a bright Sunday and Abdu'l-Baha went out with his friends driving and walking on the downs. Afterwards he gathered the servants of the house together, spoke of the dignity of labour and thanked them for their service, giving to each some remembrance of his visit. He went over the Guest house and blessed it as a centre for pilgrims from every part of the world, and said it would become indeed a House of Rest.

On the morning of the third day, a Canon of the Anglican Church met him at breakfast. The conversation turned on the reluctance of the rich to part with their possessions, Abdu'l-Baha, quoting the saying of Jesus, "How hardly shall they that have riches enter into the Kingdom of Heaven." He remarked that only when the true seeker finds that attachments to the material are keeping him from his spiritual heritage, will he gladly enter the way of renunciation. Then will the rich man joyfully share his worldly possessions with the needy. Abdu'l-Baha contrasted the unpretentious hospitality before him with the costly banquets of the wealthy, who too often sit at their feasts forgetting the hungry multitudes.

He urged his hearers to spread the light in their own homes so that finally it would illuminate the whole community.

Abdu'l-Baha then returned to London. It was the earnest wish of those who had the privilege of meeting him that his followers in other lands should know how much the Clifton people appreciated his visit and realized his spiritual power and love.

Thomas Pole.

At Byfleet.

ON the afternoon of September 9th, a number of working women of the Passmore Edwards' Settlement, who were spending their holidays with Miss Schepel and Miss Buckton at Vanners, in Byfleet, a village some twenty miles out of London, had the great privilege of meeting Abdu'l-Baha. They wrote a short record of his sayings to keep for themselves. The following is an extract:--

We gathered round him in a circle, and he made us sit beside him in the window seat. One of the members, who was ill, had a specially beautiful greeting from him. Abdu'l-Baha began by saying, as he seated himself: "Are you happy?" and our faces must have shown him that we were. He then said: "I love you all, you are the children of the Kingdom, and you are accepted of God. Though you may be poor here, you are rich in the treasures of the Kingdom. I am the Servant of the poor. Remember how His Holiness Jesus said: `Blessed are the poor!' If all the queens of the earth were gathered here, I could not be more glad!"

Abdu'l-Baha knew that we had a treasury box from which we try to help people less fortunate than ourselves. Presently he rose, and said: "You are dear to me. I want to do something for you! I cannot cook for you (he had previously seen us busy in the kitchen) but here is something for your fund." He went round the circle to each, with a beautiful smile, shaking hands with all, and giving the Baha'i greeting: "Allah'u'Abha!"

Later on he walked in the village, and many poor children came to him, and mothers with sick babies and men out of work. He spoke to them all, through an interpreter. At tea-time other friends joined us. Abdu'l-Baha liked the cottage garden at Vanners, the little orchard and the roses. He said: "This is like a Persian garden. The air is very pure."

On leaving for London he presented every one with a purple heartsease from the garden, and said again and again: "Good-bye" in English.

On the 28th September, Abdu'l-Baha again visited Vanners, the little farm house on the old royal manor that dates back to the time of Edward II. He motored down from London and stayed over night, returning on the evening of the second day.

Abdu'l-Baha was much struck during the drive by two detachments of Boy Scouts tramping the road. When told of the Scouts' motto, "Be Prepared," and that an act of kindness each day is one of their laws and that some of these boys had put out a fire and assisted at a recent railway accident, he said. "This makes me very happy."

Arriving at Vanners, he found a large, strangely mixed crowd, assembled about the gate to welcome him, from the quite poor to the wealthy who had motored over from their country places. A great number followed him and as many as could do so pressed into the garden and sat down around him. The silence was most impressive. The same attention and eagerness to hear was noticed among the people each time Abdu'l-Baha appeared in the village.

After expressing his joy at being with them, he began to speak to the little group in answer to a question about the elaborate civilization of the West.

The Captivity of Man

Abdu'l-Baha said:--"Luxuries cut off the freedom of communication. One who is imprisoned by desires is always unhappy; the children of the Kingdom have unchained themselves from their desires. Break all fetters and seek for spiritual joy and enlightenment; then, though you walk on this earth, you will perceive yourselves to be within the divine horizon. To man alone is this possible. When we look about us we see every other creature captive to his environment.

"The bird is a captive in the air and the fish a captive in the sea. Man alone stands apart and says to the elements, I will make you my servants! I can govern you! He takes electricity, and through his ingenuity imprisons it and makes of it a wonderful power for lighting, and a means of communication to a distance of thousands of miles. But man himself may become a captive to the things he has invented. His true second birth occurs when he is freed from all material things: for he only is free who is not a captive to his desires. He has then as Jesus has said, become captive to the Holy Spirit."

The Power of God

A friend asked Abdu'l-Baha how far the individual could attain to that Christ consciousness in himself of which St. Paul speaks as our hope of Glory.

Abdu'l-Baha turned with a look of great joy and said with an impressive gesture: "The bounty and power of God is limitless for each human soul. Consider what was the quickening power of the Christ when He was on earth. Look at His disciples! They were poor and uncultured men. Out of the rough fisherman He made the great Peter, and out of the poor village girl of Magdala He made one who is a power in all the world today. Many queens have reigned who are remembered by their dates in history, and nothing more is known of them. But Mary the Magdalene is greater than them all. It was she whose love strengthened the disciples when their faith was failing. What she did for the world cannot be measured. See what a divine power was enkindled in her by the power of God!"

Inspired Messengers

When asked if it would be always necessary for prophets to come from time to time--"would not the world in the course of events through progress reach to a full realization of God?"--Abdu'l-Baha replied: "Mankind needs a universal motive power to quicken it. The inspired messenger who is directly assisted by the power of God brings about universal results. Baha'u'llah rose as a light in Persia and now that light is going out to the whole world."

"Is this what is meant by the Second Coming of Christ?" "Christ is an Expression of the Divine Reality, the Single Essence and Heavenly Entity, which hath no beginning or ending. It has appearance, arising, and manifestation and setting in each one of the Cycles."

Those who have been with Abdu'l-Baha notice how, often, after speaking earnestly with people, he will suddenly turn and walk away to be alone. At such times no one follows him. On this occasion, when he finished speaking and went out through the orchard gate into the village, all were struck with his free and wonderful walk which has been described by one of our American friends as that of a shepherd or a king.

As he passed along the ragged children clustered about him by dozens, the boys saluting him as they had been taught in school, showing how instinctively they felt the greatness of his presence. Most noticeable was the silence of even the roughest men when Abdu'l-Baha appeared. One poor tramp exclaimed "He is a good man," and added, "Ay, he's suffered!"

He took particular interest in the sick, crippled and poorly nourished children. Mothers carrying their little ones followed him, and a friend explained that this great visitor had come over the seas from the Holy Land where Jesus was born.

All day long people of every condition gathered about the gate for a chance of seeing him, and more than sixty drove or cycled to Vanners to see him, many wishing to question him on some special subject. Among them were the clergy of several denominations, a head master of a boys' public school, a member of Parliament, a doctor, a famous political writer, the vice-chancellor of a University, several journalists, a well known poet, and a magistrate from London.

He will long be remembered as he sat in the bow window in the afternoon sunshine, his arm round a very ragged but very happy little boy, who had come to ask Abdu'l-Baha for sixpence for his money box and for his invalid mother, whilst round him in the room were gathered men and women discussing Education, Socialism, the first Reform Bill, and the relation of submarines and wireless telegraphy to the new era on which man is entering.

During the evening a young betrothed couple in the village, who had read some of the Baha'i books, begged permission to come to him. They entered shyly, the man, led by the girl. Abdu'l-Baha rose to greet them, and made them take a place in the circle. He talked earnestly to them upon the sacredness of marriage, the beauty of a real union, and the importance of the little child and its education. Before they left he blessed them, and touched their hair and foreheads with a Persian perfume.

Education

Abdu'l-Baha laid great stress on Education. He said "The girl's education is of more importance today than the boy's, for she is the mother of the future race. It is the duty of all to look after the children. Those without children should, if possible, make themselves responsible for the education of a child."

The condition of the destitute in the country villages as well as in London impressed Abdu'l-Baha greatly. In an earnest talk with the Rector of a Parish, Abdu'l-Baha said: "I find England awake; there is spiritual life here. But your poor are so very poor! This should not be. On the one hand you have wealth, and great luxury; on the other hand men and women are living in the extremities of hunger and want. This great contrast of life is one of the blots on the civilization of this enlightened age.

"You must turn attention more earnestly to the betterment of the conditions of the poor. Do not be satisfied until each one with whom you are concerned is to you as a member of your family. Regard each one either as a father, or as a brother, or as a sister, or as a mother, or as a child. If you can attain to this, your difficulties will vanish, you will know what to do. This is the teaching of Baha'u'llah."

The Change of Heart

To one who spoke of the people's desire to possess the land, and of the strong under-current of rebellion on the part of the labouring classes, Abdu'l-Baha said: " Fighting, and the employment of force, even for the right cause, will not bring about good results. The oppressed who have right on their side, must not take that right by force; the evil would continue. Hearts must be changed. The rich must wish to give! Life in man should be like a flame, warming all with whom it comes into contact. The spiritually awakened are like to bright torches in the sight of God, they give light and comfort to their fellows."

When asked if he did not find the manners of the English rude and awkward, compared with those of the East, Abdu'l-Baha said he had not felt this. As a nation increases in spirituality, the the manners become different.

Christ and Baha'u'llah

A friend asked how the teachings of Baha'u'llah contrasted with the teachings of Jesus Christ. "The teachings are the same." declared Abdu'l-Baha; "It is the same foundation and the same temple. Truth is one, and without division. The teachings of Jesus are in a concentrated form. Men do not agree to this day as to the meaning of many of His sayings. His teachings are as a flower in the bud. Today, the bud is unfolding into a flower! Baha'u'llah has expanded and fulfilled the teachings, and has applied them in detail to the whole world.

"There are no solitaries and no hermits among the Baha'is. Man must work with his fellows. Everyone should have some trade, or art or profession, be he rich or poor, and with this he must serve humanity. This service is acceptable as the highest form of worship."

Art

A painter asked: "Is art a worthy vocation?" Abdu'l-Baha turning to her impressively, said: "Art is worship."

An actor mentioned the drama, and its influence. "The drama is of the utmost importance." said Abdu'l-Baha. "It has been a great educational power in the past; it will be so again." He described how as a young boy he witnessed the Mystery Play of Ali's Betrayal and Passion, and how it affected him so deeply that he wept and could not sleep for many nights.

Symbols

Someone wished to know if it were a good custom to wear a symbol, as, for instance, a cross. He said: "You wear the cross for remembrance, it concentrates your thoughts; it has no magical power. Baha'is often wear a stone with the greatest name engraved on it: there is no magical influence in the stone; it is a reminder, and companion. If you are about to do some selfish or hasty action, and your glance falls on the ring on your hand, you will remember and change your intention."

Esperanto

A friend enquired concerning Baha'u'llah's prophecy in the Words of Paradise, that a universal language would be formed, and desired to know if Esperanto would be the language chosen.

"The love and effort put into Esperanto will not be lost," he answered, "but no one person can construct a Universal Language. It must be made by a Council representing all countries, and must contain words from different languages. It will be governed by the simplest rules, and there will be no exceptions; neither will there be gender, nor extra and silent letters. Everything indicated will have but one name. In Arabic there are hundreds of names for the camel! In the schools of each nation the mother tongue will be taught, as well as the revised Universal Language."

Tolstoy

The same questioner said: "I have read much of Tolstoy and I see a parallel between his teachings and yours. In one of his books he speaks of the Enigma of Life, and describes how life is wasted in our endeavour to find the Key. But Tolstoy goes on to say: 'There is a man in Persia who holds the secret.'"

"Yes," said Abdu'l-Baha, "I received a letter from Tolstoy, and in it he said that he wished to write a book upon Baha'u'llah."

Healing

A friend interested in healing quoted the words of Baha'u'llah: "If one is sick, let him go to the greatest physician."

Abdu'l-Baha said: "There is but one power which heals--that is God. The state or condition through which the healing takes place is the confidence of the heart. By some this state is reached through pills, powders, and physicians. By others through hygiene, fasting, and prayer. By others through direct perception."

On another occasion Abdu'l-Baha said with regard to the same subject, "All that we see around us is the work of mind. It is mind in the herb and in the mineral that acts on the human body, and changes its condition." The talk developed into a learned dissertation on the Philosophy of Aristotle.

Death

A friend asked: "How should one look forward to death?"

Abdu'l-Baha answered: "How does one look forward to the goal of any journey? With hope and with expectation. It is even so with the end of this earthly journey. In the next world, man will find himself freed from many of the disabilities under which he now suffers. Those who have passed on through death, have a sphere of their own. It is not removed from ours; their work, the work of the Kingdom, is ours; but it is sanctified from what we call `time and place.' Time with us is measured by the sun. When there is no more sunrise, and no more sunset, that kind of time does not exist for man. Those who have ascended have different attributes from those who are still on earth, yet there is no real separation.

"In prayer there is a mingling of station, a mingling of condition. Pray for them as they pray for you! When you do not know it, and are in a receptive attitude, they are able to make suggestions to you, if you are in difficulty. This sometimes happens in sleep. but there is no phenomenal intercourse! That which seems like phenomenal intercourse has another explanation." The questioner exclaimed; "But I have heard a voice!" Abdu'l-Baha said: "Yes, that is possible; we hear voices clearly in dreams. It is not with the physical ear that you heard; the spirit of those that have passed on are freed from sense-life, and do not use physical means. It is not possible to put these great matters into human words; the language of man is the language of children, and man's explanation often leads astray."

Someone present asked how it was that in prayer and meditation the heart often turns with instinctive appeal to some friend who has passed into the next life.

Abdu'l-Baha answered: "It is a law of God's creation that the weak should lean upon the strong. Those to whom you turn may be the mediators of God's power to you, even as when on earth. But it is the One Holy Spirit that strengthens all men." Hereupon another friend referred to the communing of Jesus on the Mount of Transfiguration with Moses and Elijah; and Abdu'l-Baha said: "The faithful are ever sustained by the presence of the Supreme Concourse. In the Supreme Concourse are Jesus, and Moses, and Elijah, and Baha'u'llah, and other supreme Souls: there, also, are the martyrs."

When asked about the individual persistence of the animal's personality after death, Abdu'l-Baha said: "Even the most developed dog has not the immortal soul of the man; yet the dog is perfect in its own place. You do not quarrel with a rose-tree because it cannot sing!"

A True Baha'i

A student of the modern methods of the higher criticism asked Abdu'l-Baha if he would do well to continue in the church with which he had been associated all his life, and whose language was full of meaning to him. Abdu'l-Baha answered: "You must not dissociate yourself from it. Know this; the Kingdom of God is not in any Society; some seekers go through many Societies as a traveller goes through many cities till he reach his destination. If you belong to a Society already do not forsake your brothers. You can be a Baha'i-Christian, a Baha'i-Freemason, a Baha'i-Jew, a Baha'i-Muhammadan. The number nine contains eight, and seven, and all the other numbers, and does not deny any of them. Do not distress or deny anyone by saying 'He is not a Baha'i!' He will be known by his deeds. There are no secrets among Baha'is; a Baha'i does not hide anything."

Spreading the Teaching

When asked by an American friend: "Which is the best way to spread the teaching?" he said: "By deeds. This way is open to all, and deeds are understood by all. Join yourselves to those who work for the poor, the weak and the unfortunate; this is greatly to be commended. To teach by words requires the skill of a wise physician. He does not offer help to those who do not want treatment. Do not press help on those who do not need your help. The work of teaching is not for all."

The following incident shows how Abdu'l-Baha's attention is given to the smallest details where others are involved. On hearing that some of his friends had come down from London, and had planned to stop the night in the village so as to be near him Abdu'l-Baha immediately made them his guests at the Inn, and being concerned for their comfort, went over personally to inspect the rooms, as the nights were getting cold.

At Brooklands

The morning of the second day, a neighbour sent over her car asking if Abdu'l-Baha would not like to take his guests to the Brooklands aviation ground. Though it was windy, an aviator was on the track, when he heard who the visitor was offered to fly for him. Abdu'l-Baha left his friends and walked out into the middle of the course, where he stood alone watching the biplane making wide circles above him.

A Hindu who was learning to fly at the school joined Abdu'l-Baha's friends and asked: "Who is the man in Eastern dress?"

When told, he exclaimed, "Oh I know him very well through his teachings, which I have studied," and immediately he went to meet Abdu'l-Baha.

They talked together for some time in Arabic, the young man showing great joy at being in his presence. He afterwards said that for many years he had longed for this moment.

While having tea out of doors, Abdu'l-Baha and the young Hindu, sitting at the head of the long benches that has been arranged, talked merrily to everyone.

Abdu'l-Baha noticed two of the airmen who were wrestling on the grounds, and when they stopped, he went to them clapping his hands and crying in English, "Bravo! Bravo! that is good exercise."

Since his return to Egypt, Abdu'l-Baha has sent a kind message of remembrance to the people of Byfleet, saying that he will never forget them.

Days in London

DURING Abdu'l-Baha's stay in Cadogan Gardens people arrived all day and every day, from early morning to nightfall, hoping for the privilege of seeing him and of hearing him talk. Many were the gatherings round the board of that hospitable house and hundreds of people were made welcome. Many came without introduction and no one was refused. Among them were clergy of various denominations, members of Parliament, magistrates, and literary men.

The visitors were not only English; numerous Persians had journeyed from Tihran and other Eastern cities to meet freely one who had so long been withheld from them by his captivity.

The editor of a journal printed in Japan, altered his return route to Tokyo in order that he might spend the night near Abdu'l-Baha, and a late visit was paid by a Zoroastrian physician of Bombay, on the eve of his return to India.

Woman's Work

Abdu'l-Baha's interest in women's work and progress is well known, and among the notable leaders who came to see him, may be mentioned Mrs. Annie Besant, President of the Theosophical Society, the organizers of various suffrage bodies, civic and philanthropic workers, the principals of several woman's colleges and lady doctors.

A spirited conversation due to the visit of an ardent suffragist will be long remembered by those who had the privilege of being present. The room was full of men and women, many Persians being seated in their familiar respectful attitude on the floor.

After contrasting the general position of the Eastern and the Western women, and then describing how in many respects the Eastern woman has the advantage of her Western sister, Abdu'l-Baha turned and said to the visitor: "Give me your reasons for believing that woman today should have the vote?"

Answer: "I believe that humanity is a divine humanity and that it must rise higher and higher; but it cannot soar with only one wing." Abdu'l-Baha expressed his pleasure at this answer, and smiling, replied: "But what will you do if one wing is stronger than the other?" Answer: "Then we must strengthen the weaker wing, otherwise the flight will always be hampered."

Abdu'l-Baha smiled and asked: "What will you say if I prove to you that the woman is the stronger wing?"

The answer came in the same bright vein: "You will earn my eternal gratitude!" at which all the company made merry.

Abdu'l-Baha then continued more seriously: "The woman is indeed of the greater importance to the race. She has the greater burden and the greater work. Look at the vegetable and the animal worlds. The palm which carries the fruit is the tree most prized by the date grower. The Arab knows that for a long journey the mare has the longest wind. For her greater strength and fierceness, the lioness is more feared by the hunter than the lion.

"The mere size of the brain has been proved to be no measure of superiority. The woman has greater moral courage than the man; she has also special gifts which enable her to govern in moments of danger and crisis. If necessary she can become a warrior."

Zenobia

Abdu'l-Baha asked the company if they remembered the story of Zenobia and of the fall of Palmyra. He then continued as follows, using his hands in the grave and simple gesticulations characteristic of him:

"There was once a Governor in Ancient Syria, who had a beautiful and clever wife. She was so capable that when the Governor died, she was made ruler in his stead. The land prospered under her sway, and men acknowledged that she was a better ruler than her husband. After a time the legions of Rome invaded the country, but again and again she drove them out with great confusion. She let down her beautiful hair, and herself rode at the head of her army, clad in a scarlet cloak, wearing a crown of gold, and wielding a two-edged sword in her hand. The Roman Caesar then withdrew his strength from five other provinces in order to subdue her. After a long and brave fight Zenobia retired into the city of Palmyra, which she strengthened with wonderful fortifications, and there she endured a siege of four months, Caesar being unable to dislodge her. The food she had stored within the walls at last was gone, and the misery of her starving and plague-stricken people compelled her to surrender.

"Caesar was full of admiration for this great woman, because of her courage and endurance, and he asked her to become his wife. But she refused, saying that she would never consent to take as her husband the enemy of her people. Thereupon, Caesar was enraged, and determined to humble her. He took her back with him in his ships to Rome. For his triumphal entry a great procession was prepared, and the streets were filled with people. In the procession came first elephants, after the elephants came the camels, after the camels came the tigers and the leopards, after the leopards came the monkeys, and lastly, after the monkeys, walked Zenobia with a gold chain round her neck. Still she carried her head high, and was firm in her determination. Nothing could break her spirit! She refused to become the Empress of Caesar, so she was thrown into a dungeon, and eventually she died."

Abdu'l-Baha ceased. Silence fell upon the room, and it was some time before it was broken.

Upon another occasion Abdu'l-Baha said to a group of friends around him: "Taken in general, women today have a stronger sense of religion than men. The woman's intuition is more correct; she is more receptive and her intelligence is quicker. The day is coming when woman will claim her superiority to man.

"Woman has everywhere been commended for her faithfulness. After the Lord Christ suffered, the disciples wept, and gave way to their grief. They thought that their hopes were shattered, and that the Cause was utterly lost, till Mary Magdalene came to them and strengthened them saying: 'Do you mourn the body of Our Lord or His Spirit? If you mourn His Spirit, you are mistaken, for Jesus lives! His Spirit will never leave us!' Thus through her wisdom and encouragement the Cause of Christ was upheld for all the days to come. Her intuition enabled her to grasp the spiritual fact."

Abdu'l-Baha then added: "But in the sight of God sex makes no difference. He or she is greatest who is nearest to God."

One morning Abdu'l-Baha, on entering the room looked about and said: "It is just like a miracle, our being here together. There is no racial, political or patriotic tie. We are drawn together by the words of Baha'u'llah, and in like manner will all the races of the earth be drawn together. Of this, rest assured!"

The True Baha'i

"I have never heard of Baha'u'llah," said a young man. I have only recently read about this movement, but I recognize the mission of Abdu'l-Baha and desire to be a disciple. I have always believed in the brotherhood of man as the ultimate solvent of all our national and international difficulties."

"It makes no difference whether you have ever heard of Baha'u'llah or not," was the answer, "the man who lives the life according to the teachings of Baha'u'llah is already a Baha'i. On the other hand a man may call himself a Baha'i for fifty years and if he does not live the life he is not a Baha'i. An ugly man may call himself handsome, but he deceives no one, and a black man may call himself white yet he deceives no one: not even himself!"

The Coming of Peace

"By what process" continued the questioner, "will this peace on earth be established? Will it come at once after a universal declaration of the Truth?"

"No, it will come about gradually," said Abdu'l-Baha. "A plant that grows too quickly lasts but a short time. You are my family" and he looked about with a smile, "my new children! if a family lives in unison, great results are obtained. Widen the circle; when a city lives in intimate accord greater results will follow, and a continent that is fully united will likewise unite all other continents. Then will be the time of the greatest results, for all the inhabitants of the earth belong to one native land."

The Pure Heart

When asked for a definition of a pure heart, Abdu'l-Baha said, "The pure heart is one that is entirely cut away from self. To be selfless is to be pure."

True Spirituality

Another morning Abdu'l-Baha began at once to speak as he joined the group of seekers. He said: "Praise be to God, this century is a glorious century; may love increase every day; may it strike fire to light the candle in the darkness, like a gift and mercy of God.

"Know, O thou possessors of insight, that true spirituality is like unto a lake of clear water which reflects the divine. Of such was the spirituality of Jesus Christ. There is another kind which is like a mirage, seeming to be spiritual when it is not. That which is truly spiritual must light the path to God, and must result in deeds. We cannot believe the call to be spiritual when there is no result. Spirit is reality, and when the spirit in each of us seeks to join itself with the Great Reality, it must in turn give life. The Jews in the time of Christ were dead, having no real life, and Jesus actually wafted a new breath into their bodies. Behold what has been accomplished since!"

Knowledge must result in Action

A representative from a well known society made reference to its meetings for the purpose of a search into the reality of truth, and Abdu'l-Baha said "I know of your work. I think a great deal of it. I know your desire is to serve mankind, and to draw together Humanity under the banner of Oneness; but its members must beware less it become only a discussion. Look about you. How many committees have been formed, and living for a little while, have died! Committees and Societies can not create or give life.

"People get together and talk, but it is God's Word alone that is powerful in its results. Consider for a moment: you would not trade together if you had no income from it and derived no benefit! Look at the followers of Christ. Their power was due to their ardour and their deeds. Every effort must have its result, else it is not a true effort. You must become the means of lighting the world of humanity. This is the infallible proof and sign. Every progress depends on two things, knowledge and practice. First acquire knowledge, and, when conviction is reached, put it into practice.

"Once a learned man journeyed to see me to receive my blessing, saying he knew and comprehended the Baha'i teachings. When I told him that he could receive the blessings of the Holy Spirit at any time when he put himself in a receptive attitude to accept them, he said he was always in a receptive attitude.

"'What would you do,' I asked 'if I were to suddenly turn and strike you?' He instantly flared with indignation and strode angrily about the room.

"After a little I went over and took his arm, saying, 'But you must return good for evil. Whether I honoured you or despised you, you should follow the teachings; now you merely read them. Remember the words of Jesus who said, 'The first shall be last, and the last first.' The man turned, shook my hand and departed, and I have since heard of many kind acts he has done."

When Abdu'l-Baha was addressed by the name of prophet, he answered, "My name is Abdu'l-Baha, the Servant of God" [literally, the Slave of Glory.]

Visit to the Lord Mayor

At the express wish of the Lord Mayor, Abdu'l-Baha paid him a visit early one morning at the Mansion House. The talk turned chiefly upon the social conditions of great cities, and Abdu'l-Baha said that London was the best regulated city he had seen.

He said: "Every man walking in the street is free as if he were in his own kingdom. There is a   Compare:--"My Name is Abdu'l-Baha. My Reality is   Abdu'l-Baha: and Service to all the human race is my perpetual   Religion.... Abdu'l-Baha is the Banner of the Most Great Peace   ...The Herald of the Kingdom is he, so that he may awaken the   people of the East and the West. The Voice of Friendship, of   Truth, and of Reconciliation is he, quickening all regions. No   name, no title will he ever have, except Abdu'l-Baha. This is my   longing. This is my Supreme height. O ye friends of God!   Abdu'l-Baha is the manifestation of Service, and not Christ. The   Servant of humanity is he, and not a chief. Summon ye the people   to the station of Service of Abdu'l-Baha and not his Christhood."   (From a letter sent to the friends in New York, January 1st, 1907.)   great spiritual light in London. The effort made for justice is real and in this country the law is the same for the poor as for the rich." He took great interest in hearing of the care that is taken of prisoners as they leave jail, and spoke of the land being happy where the magistrates are as fathers to the people.

Before Abdu'l-Baha left London, he went to an East-end hospital to visit there a young writer lying seriously ill, who was very anxious to see him.

Some Personal Characteristics

There is a note in Abdu'l-Baha's character that has not been emphasized, and with which no idea of him is complete. The impressive dignity which distinguishes his presence and bearing is occasionally lighted by a delicate and tactful humour, which is as unaffected as it is infectious and delightful.

On his last afternoon in London, a reporter called to ask him of his future plans, finding him surrounded by a number of friends who had called to bid him good-bye. When, in answer to this query, Abdu'l-Baha told in perfect English of his intention to visit Paris and go from there to Alexandria, the press representative evinced surprise at his faultless pronunciation. Thereupon Abdu'l-Baha proceeded to march with a free stride up and down the flower-scented drawing room, his Oriental garb contrasting strangely with his modern surroundings; and, to the amusement of the assembly, uttered a string of elaborate English words, laughingly ending, "Very difficult English words I speak!" Then, a moment later, with the swift transition of one who knows both how to be grave and gay, he showed himself terribly in earnest.

He had left orders that none were to be turned away, but one who had twice vainly sought his presence, and was, through some oversight, prevented from seeing him, wrote a heartbreaking letter showing that he thought himself rebuffed. It was translated by the Persian interpreter. Abdu'l-Baha at once put on his coat, and, turning towards the door, said, with an expression of unspeakable sadness, "A friend of mine has been martyred, and I am very grieved. I go out alone." and he swept down the steps. One could then see how well the title of "Master" became him.

Another phase of his character which none who saw him could ever forget was his attitude towards children who were brought to him. Many of his talks were given as he sat with his arm encircling one of them.

He invariably admonished the parents thus: "Give this child a good education; make every effort that it may have the best you can afford, so that it may be enabled to enjoy the advantage of this glorious age. Do all you can to encourage spirituality in them."

One who sought the presence of Abdu'l-Baha realized the father-like sympathy which is his. Speaking of his and others' love for Abdu'l-Baha the reply was: "I know that you love me, I can see that it is so. I will pray for you that you may be firm and serve in the Cause, becoming a true servant to Baha'u'llah. Though I go away I will always be present with you all." These words were spoken with the greatest loving sympathy and understanding of difficulties; during the moments of this little talk Abdu'l-Baha held and stroked the speaker's hands, and at the end took his head and with a gentle touch drew it to him kissing the forehead of the young man, who felt that he had found a father and a friend.

The Farewell

ON the last morning of Abdu'l-Baha's stay in London many friends gathered both at Cadogan Gardens and at the station to bid him farewell. An impressive and interesting ceremony was performed at the house by a Zoroastrian (a physician), who sent an elaborate telegram to some Parsis in Bombay, saying: "The Torch of Truth has been lighted again in the East and the West by Abdu'l-Baha." Instructed by his brethren, this follower of one of the most ancient religions in the world had brought with him a sacred oil of a rare perfume, with which he anointed the head and breast of Abdu'l-Baha, afterwards touching the hands of all present. He then placed around Abdu'l-Baha's neck and shoulders an exquisite garland of rose-buds and lilies.

The last glimpse which the friends had at Victoria Station was that of the venerable face and form standing at the window, gazing out with a look of benevolence and wonderful tenderness on those he was leaving.

From an Interview given by Abdu'l-Baha

to the Weekly Budget.

September 23rd, 1911.

SOME OF THE EXPERIENCES OF HIS

FORTY YEARS IMPRISONMENT

IN an apartment in Cadogan Gardens sits a spiritually illumined Oriental, whose recent advent in London marks the latest junction of the East and West.

The teaching of Abdu'l-Baha has already brought about the commingling of thousands of Englishmen and Englishwomen with Orientals from every quarter of the East. Upon the basis of mutual help and friendship and the worship of God, regardless of creed and denomination, they have joined hands with an earnestness and brotherly love contrary to the theories of certain cynical poets and philosophers.

Most of Abdu'l-Baha's life has been spent in an Eastern prison, which he gladly endured rather than abjure his faith, one of the tenets of which is the absolute equality of souls regardless of physical differences, such as sex and colour. He recognizes no class distinctions except those conferred by service and the spirit of brotherly love. For this and other like doctrines he was held prisoner for forty years in the fortress city of Akka, in Palestine. When I requested to talk with him, I was told to come early, and called, according, at nine o'clock, for an interview. It was already mid-day to Abdu'l-Baha who rises at four, and who had seen eighteen people before his breakfast at half-past six.

Representatives of many languages and nationalities awaited him in the drawing room.

We sat in a circle facing Abdu'l-Baha who inquired if there were any questions we would like to ask. I said my editor had sent me to ascertain something of his prison life, and Abdu'l-Baha at once related in a simple impersonal way one of the most remarkable stories conceivable.

"At nine years of age, I accompanied my father, Baha'u'llah, in his journey of exile to Baghdad, seventy of his disciples going with us. This decree of exile, after persistent persecution, was intended to effectively stamp out of Persia what the authorities considered a dangerous religion. Baha'u'llah, with his family and followers, was banished, and travelled from one place to another. When I was about twenty-five years old, we were moved from Constantinople to Adrianople, and from there went with a guard of soldiers to the fortressed city of Akka, where we were imprisoned and closely guarded."

The First Summer

"We had no communication whatever with the out-side world. Each loaf of bread was cut open by the guard to see that it contained no message. All who believed in the Baha'i manifestation, children, men and women, were imprisoned with us. There were one-hundred and fifty of us together in two rooms and no one was allowed to leave the place with the exceptions of four persons, who went to the bazaar to market each morning, under guard. The first summer was dreadful. Akka is a fever-ridden town. It was said that a bird attempting to fly over it would drop dead. The food was poor and insufficient, the water was drawn from a fever-infected well and the climate and conditions were such, that even the natives of the town fell ill. Many soldiers succumbed and eight out of ten of our guard died. During the intense heat, malaria, typhoid and dysentery attacked the prisoners, so that all, men, women and children, were sick at one time. There were no doctors, no medicines, no proper food, and no treatment of any kind.

"I used to make broth for the people, and as I had much practice, I make good broth," said Abdu'l-Baha laughingly.

At this point one of the Persians explained to me that it was on account of Abdu'l-Baha's wonderful patience, helpfulness, and endurance that he was always called "The Master." One could easily feel his mastership in his complete severance from time and place, and absolute detachment from all that even a Turkish prison could inflict.

Better Conditions

"After two years of the strictest confinement permission was granted me to find a house so that we could live outside the prison walls but still within the fortifications. Many believers came from Persia to join us but they were not allowed to do so. Nine years passed. Sometimes we were better off and sometimes very much worse. It depended on the governor, who, if he happened to be a kind and lenient ruler, would grant us permission to leave the fortification, and would allow the believers free access to visit the house; but when the governor was more rigorous, extra guards were placed around us, and often pilgrims who had come from afar were turned away."

I learned, afterwards, from a Persian, who, during these troublous times, was a member of Abdu'l-Baha's household, that the Turkish government could not credit the fact that the interest of the English and American visitors was purely spiritual and not political. Often these pilgrims were refused permission to see him, and, many times, the whole trip from America would be rewarded merely by a glimpse of Abdu'l-Baha from his prison window.

The Government thought that the tomb of the Bab, an imposing building on Mount Carmel, was a fortification erected with the aid of American money, and that it was being armed and garrisoned secretly. Suspicion grew with each new arrival, resulting in extra spies and guards.

Abdu'l-Hamid's Committee

"One year before Abdu'l-Hamid was dethroned, he sent an extremely overbearing, treacherous and insulting committee of investigation. The chairman was one of the governor's staff, Arif Bey, and with him were three army commanders varying in rank.

"Immediately upon his arrival, Arif Bey proceeded to denounce me and tried to get proof strong enough to warrant sending me to Fizan, or throwing me into the sea. Fizan is a caravan station on the boundary of Tripoli where there are no houses and no water. It is a month's journey by camel route from Akka.

"The committee twice sent for me to hear what I had to say in my own defence and twice I sent back word: 'I know your purpose, I have nothing to say.'

"This so infuriated Arif Bey that he declared he would return to Constantinople and bring back an order from the Sultan to have me hanged at the gate of Akka. He and his committee set sail with their report containing the following accusations:--Abdu'l-Baha is establishing a new nation of which he is to be the king; Abdu'l-Baha is uplifting the banner of a new religion; Abdu'l-Baha has built or caused to be built fortifications in Haifa, a neighbouring village, and is buying up all the surrounding lands.'

"About this time an Italian ship appeared in the harbour sent by order of the Italian Consul. It had been planned that I was to escape on it by night. The Baha'is in Akka implored me to go but I sent this message to the captain: 'The Bab did not run away: Baha'u'llah did not run away; I shall not run away, so the ship sailed away after waiting three days and three nights.

"It was while the Sultan's committee of investigation was homeward bound that the first shell was dropped into Abdu'l-Hamid's camp and the first gun of freedom was fired into the home of despotism. That was God's gun," said Abdu'l-Baha, with one of his wonderful smiles.

"When the committee reached the Turkish capital, they had more urgent things to think of. The city was in a state of uproar and rebellion, and the committee, as members of the government staff, were delegated to investigate the insurrection. Meanwhile the people were establishing a constitutional government and Abdu'l-Hamid was given no chance to act."

The Release

"With the advent of the Young Turks' supremacy, realized through the Society of Union and Progress, all the political prisoners of the Ottoman Empire were set free. Events took the chains from my neck and placed them about Hamid's; Abdu'l-Baha came out of prison and Abdu'l-Hamid went in!"

"What became of the committee?" asked someone, breaking the deep silence that followed the recital of this thrilling page of history. "Arif Bey," continued Abdu'l-Baha, "was shot with three bullets, the general was exiled, the next in rank died, and the third ran away to Cairo, where he sought and received help from the Baha'is."

"Will you tell us how you felt while in prison and how you regard your freedom?" I asked. "We are glad that you are free."

"Thank you," he said graciously, and continuing--

"Freedom is not a matter of place. It is a condition. I was thankful for the prison, and the lack of liberty was very pleasing to me, for those days were passed in the path of service, under the utmost difficulties and trials, bearing fruits and results.

"Unless one accepts dire vicissitudes, he will not attain. To me prison is freedom, troubles rest me, death is life, and to be despised is honour. Therefore, I was happy all that time in prison. When one is released from the prison of self, that is indeed release, for that is the greater prison. When this release takes place, then one cannot be outwardly imprisoned. When they put my feet in stocks, I would say to the guard, `You cannot imprison me, for here I have light and air and bread and water.

There will come a time when my body will be in the ground, and I shall have neither light nor air nor food nor water, but even then I shall not be imprisoned.' The afflictions which come to humanity sometimes tend to centre the consciousness upon the limitations, and this is a veritable prison. Release comes by making of the will a Door through which the confirmations of the Spirit come."

This sounded so like the old theology that the modern in me rose doubting if the discipline could be compensated for by the effort. "What do you mean by the confirmations of the Spirit?"

"The confirmations of the Spirit are all those powers and gifts which some are born with (and which men sometimes call genius), but for which others have to strive with infinite pains. They come to that man or woman who accepts his life with radiant acquiescence."

Radiant acquiescence--that was the quality with which we all suddenly seemed inspired as Abdu'l-Baha bade us good-bye.

It was a remarkable experience, hearing one who had passed along the prison path for forty years declare "There is no prison but the prison self;" and it drove conviction to one's mind as this white-robed messenger from the East pointed the way out,--not by the path called "Renunciation," but "Unattachment;" Radiant Acquiescence--the Shining Pathway out of the "greater prison of self" as Abdu'l-Baha so beautifully terms those bars that keep us from our fulfillment.

Isabel Fraser.

A Loving Farewell Greeting.

After leaving London and during his two months stay in Paris, Abdu'l-Baha frequently sent back messages to his English friends, some of whom journeyed over to take advantage of the conferences there. On the eve of his departure for Alexandria, he gave the following admonitory farewell to the people of England and France.

"Work," he said unceasingly, "for the day of Universal Peace. Strive always that you may be united. Kindness and love in the path of service must be your means.

"I bid a loving farewell to the people of France and England. I am very much pleased with them. I counsel them that they may day by day strengthen the bond of love and amity to this end,--that they may become the sympathetic embodiment of one nation.-- That they may extend themselves to a Universal Brotherhood to guard and protect the interests and rights of all the nations of the East,--that they may unfurl the Divine Banner of justice,--that they may treat each nation as a family composed of the individual children of God and may know that before the sight of God the rights of all are equal. For all of us are the children of one Father. God is at peace with all his children; why should they engage in strife and warfare among themselves? God is showering down kindness; why should the inhabitants of this world exchange unkindness and cruelty?"

"I will pray for you that you may be illumined with the Light of the Eternal."

Greetings by Abdu'l-Baha from Paris to London. October 1911. Spoken to Mrs. Enthoven for conveyance to all the friends, and now written from memory.

ABDU'L-BAHA sent his greetings to all, begging all to go on acquiring strength in their belief and courage in its proclamation.

He spoke much of the pleasure he had felt in the atmosphere of England. He said there was a strength of purpose in the English people and a firmness which he liked and admired, There was honesty and uprightness. They were slow in starting a new idea, but, when they did, it was only because their minds and common-sense had told them that the idea was sound.

The English as a nation had pleased him greatly.

Believers, he added, must show their belief in their daily lives, so that the world might see the light shining in their faces. A bright and happy face cheers people on their way. If you are sad, and pass a child who is laughing, the child, seeing your sad face, will cease to laugh, not knowing why. If the day be dark, how much a gleam of sunshine is prized; so let believers wear smiling happy faces, gleaming like sunshine in the darkness. Let the Light of Truth and Honesty shine from them, so that all who behold them may know that their word in business or pleasure will be a word to trust and depend upon.

Forget self and work for the whole race. Remember always that one is working for the world, not for a town or even for a country; because, as all are brethren, so every country is, as it were, one's own.

Remember, above all, the teaching of Baha'u'llah concerning gossip and unseemly talk about others. Stories repeated about others are seldom good. A silent tongue is the safest. Even good may be harmful, if spoken at the wrong time, or to the wrong person.

Finally Abdu'l-Baha sent his greetings and blessings to all, and assured me he was constantly thinking and praying for all.

To a gentleman who was questioning him, he remarked "The beginnings of all great religions were pure; but priests, taking possession of the minds of the people, filled them with dogmas and superstitions, so that religion became gradually corrupt. I come to teach no new religion. `My only desire is, through the blessing of God, to show the road to the Great Light." Touching the gentleman gently on his shoulder, as a loving father might touch a son, he went on to say, "I am no Prophet, only a man like yourself."

November 26th, 1911.

Message to the London Baha'is for the

Day of Abdu'l-Baha.

Specially given to Mrs. Enthoven.

GOOD NEWS! GOOD NEWS!

The doors of the Kingdom of God are open!

GOOD NEWS! GOOD NEWS! Armies of Angels are descending from Heaven!

GOOD NEWS! GOOD NEWS! The Sun of Truth is rising!

GOOD NEWS! GOOD NEWS! Heavenly food is being sent from above!

GOOD NEWS! GOOD NEWS! The Trumpet is sounding!

GOOD NEWS! GOOD NEWS! The Banner of the Great Peace is floating far and wide!

GOOD NEWS! GOOD NEWS! The Light of the Lamp of the Oneness of Humanity is shining bright!

GOOD NEWS! GOOD NEWS! The fire of the Love of God is blazing!

GOOD NEWS! GOOD NEWS! The Holy Spirit is being outpoured!

GOOD NEWS! GOOD NEWS! For Everlasting Life is here! O Ye that sleep, Awake! O ye heedless ones, Learn wisdom! O

Blind, receive your sight! O Deaf, Hear! O Dumb, Speak! O Dead, Arise!

Be Happy!

Be Happy!

Be full of Joy! This is the day of the Proclamation of the Bab! It is the Festival of the Forerunner of the Blessed Beauty (Baha'u'llah). It is the day of the dawning of the Morning of Guidance.

Printed in Great Britain
by Amazon

49325425R00071